North London resident, 14 year-old Olivia Daly, has a passion for cooking and qualified with a certificate in level 2 Food and Hygiene (needed to bake as a trade) at just 12 years of age.

Diagnosed with Asperger syndrome, Olivia has a tendency to fixate, with unbounded enthusiasm, on things about which she is passionate which explains early morning wake up calls to prove croissants and a highly stocked kitchen at her home in London. Necessary changes in her own diet prompted her to experiment and create healthy recipes as well as adapt those she loves into healthier versions of themselves - her gluten-free chocolate cake is sublime.

Her cookbook is filled with gluten-free, sugar-free and some dairy-free recipes and, for ease of use, it has been divided into Breakfast; Snacks; Mains and Sides and has suggested diet plans so that you have something healthy to eat each day of the week and for each meal of the day.

The nutritional information has been contributed by Andy Daly, Olivia's mum, currently a student at the Institute for Optimum Nutrition. She gives grateful thanks to Functional Medicine practitioner, Pete Williams, who has guided her and approved all the information provided.

Photographer, Aruna Khanzada, a foodie in her own right, has generously donated her photography which so brilliantly captures each mouthwatering morsel.

All proceeds raised from the sale of the books will go to Shaare Zedek Medical Centre, a renowned not-for-profit hospital in Jerusalem which offers world class medical care to all people regardless of religion, nationality or means. Its benefactors around the world help fund its equipment, supplies and research. Your act of buying this book is helping to saves lives.

Shaare Zec
for Jerusalem's hospital

GW00721838

Published by Homemade Books Publishing in 2014
87 Gloucester Ave, London, NW1 8LB
In association with Shaare Zedek UK
www.shaarezedek.org.uk. Tel. +44 208 2018933
766 Finchley Road London, NW11 7TH

ISBN 978-0-9561764-5-15

Recipes by Olivia Daly, Andrea Daly and
contributions from Aruna Khanzada
Photography by Aruna Khanzada
Design and formatting by Aruna Khanzada and Stephanie Kronson
Proof reading by Stephanie Kronson, Andrea Daly and Sybil Benn
Editing and copy by Stephanie Kronson (Shaare Zedek UK)
Title by Denis Daly
Food preparation by Olivia Daly, Andrea Daly and Carol Lambert
Food styling by Aruna Kahnzada and Andrea Daly
Nutritional information by Andrea Daly and Pete Williams
SHAARE ZEDEK UK©2014

Printed by Hexagon Print, England

Table of Contents

Sides

Sauces

Cakes and Desserts_____ 67
(all gluten-free and sugar-free)

Midwives in the Neonatal Intensive Care Unit,
Shaare Zedek Medical Centre

Dear Reader

I think this book is very much about quality rather than quantity.

I have included enough recipes to keep you well fed... ish throughout the week
Things like muesli, you make once and then you can keep in an airtight container for a couple of weeks.
The breads, muffins and rolls will stay fresh for at least 4 days and you can make a few loaves and rolls at once and freeze them.

This book simply divides into:

❋ Breakfast...to keep you full and focused
❋ Snacks... to be eaten mid morning or mid afternoon or ya know, whenever you get cravings for something sweet
❋ Mains and Sides... mostly my mum's recipes - hard for me to get used to but learning to cook them was a cultural experience nonetheless
❋ Cakes and Desserts.. YUM...

This isn't a fad diet book. It's a book about healthy eating and having a laugh. Remember food makes us full of zest and liveliness, especially sugary foods , but we need to stay grounded. We don't exactly want to be on another planet. Easier said than done for me because I have Asperger Syndrome and am always in cyberspace! Also if there is too much input and not enough output we will be out of sync and then of course all the extra energy will eventually get stored in our bodies as fat....thunder-thighs, bingo-wings, spare tyre, multiple chins ...the list is endless. All of this will happen much less quickly if we ingest the wonder-foods in this book. They are all nourishing and should make you feel healthier, focuseder (is that a word? You know what I mean) and full of exuberance, as sugary foods make you tired, less focused and grumpy. I should know because I used to be seriously overweight (at 72.5 kg and with a BMI of 25.8 when it should have been between 18.5 and 24.9). I was also on the verge of hyperinsulimia. My insulin was 19 and should have been less than 10. It is now 8.2. I managed to bust the junk and achieve all this by eating the healthy treats and other foods in this book. I lost 12kg in 6 months!! Of course I had my blips along the way, and always will, but it was always easy to get back on track with these recipes. So wishing you readers and aspiring chefs happy reading and pleasurable cheffing.

Lots of love,

Shaare Zedek UK

for Jerusalem's hospital with a heart

www.shaarezedek.org.uk

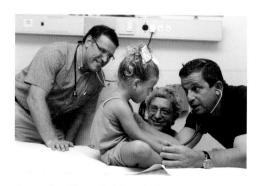

Images from Shaare Zedek Medical Centre

BREAKFAST

What About...

Mon: Liv's Granola with nut milk or Cashew Cream and blueberries

Tue: Liv's Almond Bread, toasted with Liv's Sugar-Free Jam

Wed: Liv's Almond Bread, toasted with Liv's Nutella

Thu: Oats for Groats

Fri: Coconut Apple Rings with plain Greek yoghurt

Sat: Scrambled eggs on Liv's Almond Bread, toasted

Sun: Pancakes

Liv's Granola

I make a whole batch of this stuff and keep it in an airtight container for 2 weeks if my brother Bobby doesn't get his hands on it.

INGREDIENTS

3 cups of gluten-free rolled oats
1 cup of nuts (pecans/almonds/pistachios/hazelnuts/walnuts/etc)
1/2 a cup of sweetener (maple syrup/honey/brown rice syrup)
1/4 of a cup of oil (canola/melted coconut oil)
pinch of salt
1 egg white

OPTIONAL INGREDIENTS

1 cup unsweetened coconut flakes, 1 cup dried fruit, 1 tablespoon mixed spices, (cinnamon, ginger, nutmeg, etc), 1 cup dark chocolate chips, pumpkin seeds and other assorted seeds

METHOD

Preheat oven to 160°c fan. Measure oats, nuts, salt, spices, and optional ingredients (if using) into a large bowl. In a separate small bowl, mix 1 slightly beaten egg white with oil and sweetener. Add liquid mixture to dry ingredients, stir well. If you use some of the optional ingredients and you find the mixture quite dry, add some more wet ingredients such as sweetener or oil. Spread onto a large baking sheet. Bake for 30-45 minutes, or until golden brown and fragrant. Let it cool completely and store in an airtight container until eaten.

Liv's Gluten Free Almond Loaf

I make a couple of loaves at a time and freeze one of them. If we manage to control ourselves, the loaf lasts 4 days sealed in an air-tight container.

INGREDIENTS

2 cups (100 g) ground almonds

1 cup (125 g) tapioca flour

1/2 cup (72.5 g) potato starch

1/2 cup (72.5 g) teff flour

1/4 cup (56.25 g) unsalted butter, melted

1/4 cup (125 ml) maple syrup

2 tbsp gluten free yeast

(Not all yeasts are gluten free,

so Google to check if yours is)

2 teaspoons salt

1 ½ cups (375 ml) warm water

2 tsp xantham gum

1/2 cup (50 g) desiccated coconut

3 eggs, slightly beaten

1 tbsp cinnamon

NUTRI-FACTs
Natural saturated fats, like butter, are good for you and better than margarine. This bread has protein in it which helps stabilize blood sugar levels.

METHOD

Preheat oven to 150 °c fan (170 ° normal). In a mixing bowl, mix yeast with the water and leave aside for 2 min. In another bowl, mix ground almonds, tapioca flour, potato starch, teff flour, melted butter, maple syrup, xanthan gum, eggs, cinnamon,and coconut. Add this mix to water and yeast, mixing well by hand. Add salt and whisk till fluffy . Pour mix into a well greased loaf tin and leave to prove for 45 minutes, or until the mix has doubled in size. Sprinkle with chopped pumpkin seeds.

Place cake in oven for 45 minutes. Tip: tap top if it's hollow - it's ready

Pancakes

" The laziest man I ever met put popcorn in his pancakes so they would turn over by themselves." (W.C Fields)

INGREDIENTS

50 g cornflour

50 g quinoa flour or any other gluten-free flour

50 g xylitol or coconut palm sugar

200 ml almond or macadamia nut milk, or skimmed or semi-skimmed milk, if you prefer

2½ tbsp water

1 medium egg

coconut oil for frying

NUTRI-FACT ✳

The carbohydrates in the pancakes are slow-re-leasing and combined with the blueberries and the nut cream, they will provide a nutritious breakfast and will ensure balanced blood sugar levels, making you feel less hungry.

METHOD

Whisk all the ingredients (except the oil) in a blender until completely mingled in. Melt the coconut oil and tip in a bit of the mixture until you think it is thick enough for one pancake, depending on whether you like them thick or thin. Spread it evenly and cook it for about 45 seconds. Then flip it or, if you are a bit clumsy, turn it gently with a spatula and cook both sides until golden. Serve with cashew nut cream or crème fraîche and blueberries. (*Cashew Cream Recipe p.22)*

Scrambled Eggs on my Gluten Free Almond Loaf, Toasted

" It may be the cock that crows, but it is the hen that lays the eggs."
(Margaret Thatcher)

INGREDIENTS

2 free range organic eggs

handful of chives, chopped

1 slice of my gluten-free almond bread,toasted

METHOD

Whisk the eggs and add the chives. Gently heat a teaspoon of butter and add the
eggs, folding gently until soft and creamy-like. Serve on my gluten-free bread
toasted.

NUTRI-FACT ✻
Did you know that eggs are one of the few foods considered to be a complete protein because they contain
all 9 essential amino acids? Amino acids are considered
the "building blocks" for the body because they help
form protein.

Oats for Groats

I love oats cooked with coconut milk and sweetened with coconut nectar made from coconut blossom or with date syrup. As oat groats take much longer to cook than rolled and flattened oats, it is really worth cooking larger quantities and keeping extra portions in the fridge to reheat as and when needed. Oat groats don't just have to be eaten at breakfast. The cooked grain is great added to soups and stews.

INGREDIENTS (makes 2-3 portions)

1 cup oat groats

3 cups water

salt to taste

coconut milk to taste

A drizzle of coconut nectar

or date syrup to taste.

NUTRI-FACTs ✳

Oats has beneficial soluble fibre and a great amino acid balance and coconut milk is rich in vitamins C, E, B1, B3, B5 and B6 and minerals including iron, and selenium.

METHOD

In a pan, combine the oats and water and salt. Bring to the boil and then simmer, stirring from time to time to ensure it doesn't stick and burn. Cook until it thickens and the grain is soft (around 30 - 40 minutes). Put in individual bowls. Add coconut milk to taste (bear in mind that the milk is quite rich so don't overdo it!). Drizzle the coconut nectar or date syrup to taste.

Coconut Apple Rings

" And when you crush an apple with your teeth, say to it in your heart: Your seeds shall live in my body/ And the buds of your tomorrow shall blossom in my heart/ And your fragrance shall be my breath/ And together we shall rejoice through all seasons" (Khalil Gibran)

These are great for Rosh Hashanah and definitely a perfect fried treat at Chanukah

INGREDIENTS (serves 4)
4 Golden Delicious apples, peeled and cored, and sliced into rings
1 tbsp coconut oil for frying
1 tsp cinnamon
small handful chopped walnuts or pecan nuts
honey (optional)
full fat Greek yoghurt (optional)

METHOD
Heat the coconut oil and fry the apple rings, adding about a tablespoon of water to soften them. Turn them and fry until slightly browned and soft. To serve, sprinkle with cinnamon and chopped walnuts or pecan nuts, and, if desired, drizzle some honey over the top. Or serve with full fat Greek yoghurt as a tasty, nutritious breakfast meal with some of my homemade granola sprinkled on top.

NUTRI-FACT ❋
Apples have huge health benefits. These are only some of them! They can help prevent Alzheimer's, protect against Parkinson's, curb all sorts of cancers, decrease the risk of diabetes, reduce cholesterol, prevent gallstones, neutralize Irritable Bowel Syndrome, detoxify the liver and prevent constipation.

Liv's Nutella

INGREDIENTS

2 cups blanched hazelnuts
1/2 (120 ml) cup maple syrup
1/3 (42 g) cup cocoa powder (2/3 cup if wanted more chocolaty)
2 tbsp hazelnut oil
1 tsp vanilla extract
1/3 tsp salt

METHOD

Mix hazelnuts on high speed in a food processor until it is a smooth, loose paste, like peanut butter (yes if you leave out all the other ingredients and steps it's hazelnut butter). You can taste it at this stage but it will be hot. Chuck in the rest of the ingredients and mix till it's fully mixed, and looks somewhat like Nutella. You can taste it now but, again, it will be quite hot. Let it cool, and put in jars, and keep at room temperature for 1 month.

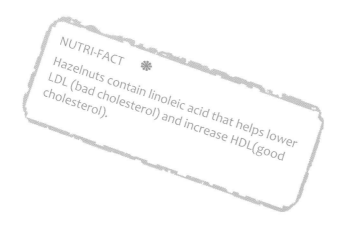

NUTRI-FACT ✳
Hazelnuts contain linoleic acid that helps lower LDL (bad cholesterol) and increase HDL(good cholesterol).

Liv's sugar-free Strawberry Jam

"Strawberry Fields forever...."

John Lennon (attributed to the John Lennon and Paul McCartney writing partnership)

I wing it when it comes to the fruit, so if you feel like it you can add more fruit and less sugar, but then you might need more pectin. You can also try it with other fruits, such as raspberries. If the fruit you are using has high pectin, you will have to omit the pectin.

INGREDIENTS

450 g strawberries, hulled,

500 g xylitol

juice of 1/2 a lemon

Pectin (follow packet instructions)

METHOD

Put strawberries into a pan, with the xylitol, lemon juice, and pectin. Heat gently on low heat, stirring slowly until xylitol has dissolved. Boil steadily for 4 minutes or until setting point is reached (you can test this by putting a saucer/plate in the freezer before making the jam , spooning a blob of jam onto it, and putting the saucer/ plate back into the freezer to cool. Then take it out and smush your finger across the jam, and if it wrinkles, and doesn't break, it's set). Remove from pan, take off scum, leave to cool, then put in jars. Jars must be thoroughly sterilized IMMEDIATELY before use. I just stick them in the dishwasher on 65 °c. **Fill them straight away then seal the jars tightly** and store for up to 3 weeks in a fridge.

Nut Milks

To make these milks, you need to blend all the ingredients in a high speed blender until smooth. Then filter them through a muslin bag (I use a dry dish cloth) or a fine strainer. They can be stored for up to two days in the fridge in an airtight container.

ALMOND NUT MILK

150 g raw almonds soaked for 6 hours, or overnight, and drained

800 ml-1 litre filtered water

MACADAMIA NUT MILK

200 g raw macadamia nuts soaked for 6 hours, or overnight and drained

800 ml-1 litre filtered water

BRAZIL NUT MILK

150 g raw Brazil nuts soaked for 6 hours, or overnight and drained

800 ml-1 litre filtered water

Cashew Cream with Vanilla

INGREDIENTS

150 g raw cashews, soaked for an hour and drained

70-130 ml filtered water

1 tsp vanilla extract

METHOD

Drain the nuts and place into the blender. Add 70 ml of the water and blend, adding more water as required to make a smooth cream. Add the vanilla and blend for a few more seconds.

SNACKS

How about...

I was going to suggest daily snacks but it was too hard to choose - rather make a whole batch of stuff like the ginger cookies, No-Bake Granola Bars and Paleo Rolls (which you can freeze and are great with savoury or sweet fillings depending on your mood); then another week bake up some Almond Shortbread and Sweet Potato muffins. The Chocolate Dipped Strawberries are delicious on a weekend.

No-Bake Granola Bars

"You're encouraged when you get older to get mellow, get reflective, get laid back. I don't understand why. I still love music like this loud guitar music, punk rock, garage rock...whatever you want to call it...now I'm supposed to make granola folk music. That doesn't make sense to me." (Steve Wyn)

INGREDIENTS

2 ½ cups rolled oats
1 cup pumpkin seeds
1/2 cup chopped 85% cocoa chocolate
2/3 cup organic peanut butter
2/3 cup maple syrup
pinch of salt
1/2 teaspoon pure orange oil extract

METHOD

In a large bowl, mix oats, pumpkin seeds and chopped dark chocolate and put aside. In a separate bowl whisk together peanut butter, maple syrup and pure orange oil. Pour into the oat mixture and mix well until it is sticky. If it is dry add a little bit more maple syrup. Press in a shallow baking dish lined with baking parchment, and cover. Refrigerate for 4 hours. Cut into squares and keep refrigerated until eaten.

Almond Shortbread

" There's a lot of fantasy about what Scotland is, and the shortbread tins, and that sort of thing." (Sean Connery)

INGREDIENTS

75 g coconut oil

75 g xylitol

75 g ground almonds

150 g quinoa or buckwheat flour

1 large handful flaked almonds

METHOD

Line a baking tray with baking parchment and pre-heat the oven to 180 °c. Mix the coconut oil and xylitol until creamy. Rub the ground almonds and flour into the mixture with your fingertips until the mixture resembles breadcrumbs. Pat the mixture evenly into the baking tray so that it is about 1/2 inch thick, sprinkle with flaked almonds and bake until brown…about 20 minutes. Allow to cool and then cut into squares and store in an airtight container.

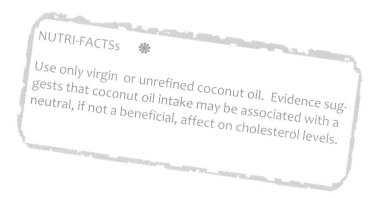

NUTRI-FACTSs ✳

Use only virgin or unrefined coconut oil. Evidence suggests that coconut oil intake may be associated with a neutral, if not a beneficial, affect on cholesterol levels.

NUTRI-FACTs ✳

Almonds, pecans and walnuts have cholesterol-lowering benefits and contain healthy fats and are also sources of fibre, protein, iron and zinc. Quinoa flour's rich in protein and contains no gluten. Coconut palm sugar contains quite a bit of the nutrients found in the coconut palm such as iron, zinc, calcium and potassium so it doesn't supply " empty calories". Like honey, it's healthier than refined sugar. Cinnamon, cloves and ginger have many therapeutic properties. Cinnamon and cloves can lower blood sugar because they contain a compound that tells the cells in the body to absorb blood sugar.

Gluten and Sugar Free Spicy Ginger Oat Cookies

"I often quote myself. It adds spice to my conversation."
George Bernard Shaw

INGREDIENTS

1/4 cup almond flour (or ground almonds)
1/2 cup quinoa flour
1/2 tsp bicarbonate of soda
1 tsp ground cinnamon
3/4 cup unsalted butter
1 cup coconut palm sugar
1 large egg, room temperature
2 tsp _pure_ vanilla extract, not essence or
1 tsp vanilla bean paste (my favourite) or 1 vanilla pod
3 cups uncooked gluten-free porridge oats (not oatmeal)
1 tsp ground ginger
1/4 or 1/3 tsp ground cloves
1/4 cup pecans or walnuts (or a mix), chopped (optional)

NUTRI-FACT

Don't buy synthetic vanilla extract; get the real extract as the synthetic ones are often wood, which has vanillin (similar to vanilla), soaked in alcohol and water rather than vanilla pods soaked in alcohol and water)

METHOD

Preheat oven to 200 °C. Cream butter and coconut palm sugar until light and fluffy (it does get hard, and after a while, you can use your hands to break up the butter and kind of melt it). Add the egg and vanilla and mix well. Add the flours, bicarbonate, spices, and oats, and fold to combine. Lastly, fold in the nuts. Divide dough into balls using a table-spoon. Flatten slightly. Bake for 10 minutes (they may look slightly underdone, but that's a good thing, as when you cool them, the residual heat from the tray will carry on cooking them a little longer, thus cooking them to perfection). Cool for a bit. Serve warm with vanilla ice cream (completely optional, but ya know, that's just what I would do because that's me).

Sweet Potato Muffins

" Two old Bachelors were living in one house; One caught a Muffin, the other caught a Mouse." (Edward Lear)

INGREDIENTS

1 large sweet potato

1/2 cup coconut oil

1/2 cup almond milk (*see recipe p 22*)

3/4 cup xylitol or coconut blossom nectar, plus 2 extra tablespoons for brushing the muffins

1 teaspoon pure vanilla extract (the one I use is Nielsen Massey)

1 cup quinoa flour

1 cup buckwheat flour

1 tsp xantham gum

2 tsp baking powder

2 tsp bicarbonate of soda

1 ½ tbsp Chinese five-spice powder

1/2 tsp salt

METHOD

Preheat the oven to 205 °c and bake the baked potato until soft and squishy, about 1 hour. Cool it completely. Peel it and mash the flesh in a mixing bowl with a fork. Whisk the coconut oil, almond milk, coconut nectar or xylitol, and vanilla into the sweet potato. In a separate bowl, mix together the dry ingredients and then fold them into the wet ingredients. Line a 12-cup muffin tin with cup case liners and distribute the muffin batter among the cups. Bake for 20 to 25 minutes, or until a knife inserted in the centre comes out clean, brushing the tops with extra coconut nectar during the last 5 minutes of baking. Cool before serving.

Fudgy Date Brownies

"All you need is love. But a little chocolate now and then doesn't hurt."   (Charles M. Schultz)

INGREDIENTS

1 cup pitted Medjool dates
3/4 cup hot water
3/4 cup almond flour
1/2 cup unsweetened
Cocoa powder
1/2 tsp. baking powder
2 tbsp coconut palm
nectar
 2 tsp vanilla extract
Pinch of sea salt

NUTRI-FACT ✳
Cocoa is high in antioxidants and is a "good mood food" because it increases serotonin levels in the brain, which is one of our " feel good hormones".

METHOD

Preheat oven to 175 °c. Pour the hot water over the dates in a bowl and leave for 10 minutes. Drain the water from the dates and place the dates in a blender and pulverise. Add the almond flour, cocoa powder, baking powder, coconut palm nectar, vanilla and salt to the food processor or blender and process until smooth. Spread the mixture a baking tray, greased with coconut oil. Bake for 20 minutes, and allow to cool before cutting. Cut into 16 square pieces and store in an airtight container in the refrigerator for up to 5 days.

Chocolate dipped Strawberries and Nuts

"The ultimate definition of oxymoron...the juxtaposition of the seemingly contradictory...seemingly because they're both good for you!"
(MOI, Olivia Daly)

INGREDIENTS

100 g good dark quality chocolate, broken into pieces
75 g shelled mixed nuts
1 punnet strawberries

METHOD

Line two baking trays with baking parchment. Melt the chocolate by putting it in a metal or glass bowl that fits the rim of a saucepan half-filled with boiling water, but does not touch it, stirring occasionally. Tip the nuts into the melted chocolate, stirring to coat. Place them on the trays, spreading them out so they do not touch and then refrigerate until hardened completely. Semi-dip the strawberries into the melted chocolate, tip down, and then spread them out on a separate baking tray and refrigerate until hardened.

Aruna's Snack Rolls

Aruna found the recipe for these paleo rolls on the Net and put them on my blog forum. They're yummy as a snack with a nut butter or my nutella or strawberry jam and are the perfect buns for the burgers.

INGREDIENTS

1 cup tapioca flour (starch)

1/4 – 1/3 cup coconut flour

1 teaspoon sea salt

1/2 cup warm water

1/2 cup olive oil

1 large egg, whisked

METHOD

Preheat oven to 175 °c.   Combine the tapioca flour (you can substitute arrow-root flour/starch) with the salt and 1/4 cup of the coconut flour in a medium bowl. Mix well. Pour in oil and warm water and stir. Add the whisked egg and continue mixing until well combined. If the mixture is too thin you should add one or two more tablespoons of coconut flour – one tablespoon at a time – until the mixture is a soft but somewhat sticky dough. Use a spatula or large spoon to scoop out about two tablespoons of the dough and roll into balls. You will be making about 10 rolls. Use extra tapioca flour in the palms of your hands so the dough does not stick. Place each roll of dough onto a greased baking pan, or parchment paper. Bake for 35 minutes.

MAINS AND SIDES

Why not try?

Mon lunch: Chicken Waldorf Salad and a slice of Liv's Almond Loaf , toasted
Mon supp: Turkey Meatballs with Vegetable Quinoa
Tue lunch: Tuna 'Colette' Salad and a slice of Liv's Almond Loaf , toasted
Tue supp: Burgers with Sweet Potato Chips
Wed lunch: Mung bean soup and a slice of Liv's almond loaf, toasted
Wed supp: Salmon Teriyaki with Basmati rice and steamed vegies
Thu lunch: Salmon Fishcakes with buttered spinach
Thu supp: Polenta/Quinoa Chicken Fingers with Blanched Greens;
Fri lunch: Quick and Easy Platter
Fri supp: Chicken Chasseur and basmati rice
Sat lunch: Buttered Spinach (make into an omelette)
Sat supp :   Vegetable Quinoa
Sun lunch: Steamed Cod with green salad and Baby potatoes
Sun supp: Mung Bean Soup, again with toast

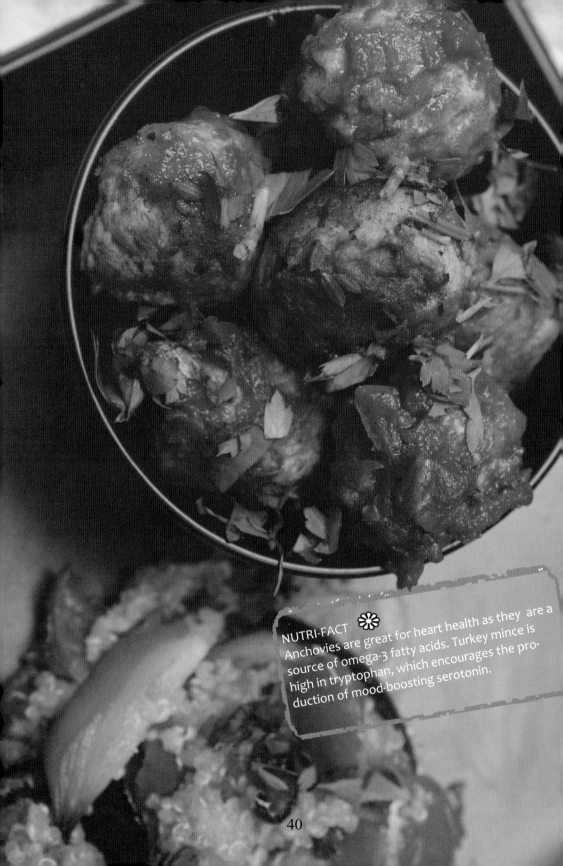

NUTRI-FACT ✤
Anchovies are great for heart health as they are a source of omega-3 fatty acids. Turkey mince is high in tryptophan, which encourages the production of mood-boosting serotonin.

Turkey Meatballs

"From a man who's eaten his fair share? I think it's all about the ...., ****, what's the secret to a good meatball? I have no idea. I like a lumpy ball, personally." (Daniel Holzman, The Meatball Shop)

INGREDIENTS (serves 4)

50 g tin anchovies in olive oil, finely chopped, oil reserved
500 g turkey mince
1 egg, beaten
2 crushed garlic cloves
1 ½ tsp each of fennel seeds, crushed and dried oregano
1 onion, finely chopped
2 tbsp tomato purée
pinch of chilli flakes
2 x 400 g tins chopped tomatoes
100 ml white wine

METHOD

Chuck in a bowl and combine anchovies, egg, turkey mince, garlic and oregano and then shape into about 24 balls. Heat the reserved oil and fry them for 8 to 10 minutes, turning a few times, until browned all over, then transfer to a plate. Add the onion and fennel seeds to the pan and cook for a further 5 minutes and then the tomato puree and cook for 2 more minutes. Add the chilli flakes, tomatoes and wine and simmer for 5 minutes returning the meatballs to the pan and cooking for 10 more minutes, turning once. I like this served with my Vegetable Quinoa (see recipe p.48)

Burgers

"It is the Americans who have managed to crown minced beef as hamburger, and to send it round the world so that even the fussy French have taken to ' le boeuf haché, le hambourgaire"
(Julia Child, American cookery expert)

INGREDIENTS (Serves 6)

500 g organic lean beef
1 small red onion, finely diced
1/2 tsp ground coriander
1/2 tsp ground cumin
1 tsp salt
ground black pepper
2 tbsp chopped flat-leaf parsley
coconut oil for frying

METHOD

Mix all the ingredients and roll into 6-8 balls and flatten into burger shapes, then fry in a little coconut oil for 15 to 20 minutes, turning halfway, until both sides are browned and the burgers are cooked through.

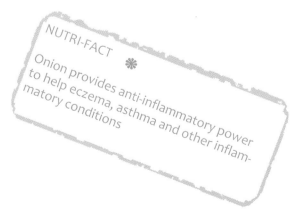

NUTRI-FACT

Onion provides anti-inflammatory power to help eczema, asthma and other inflammatory conditions

Salmon Teriyaki

INGREDIENTS (Serves 4)

4 organic salmon fillets, skin on
2 tbsp mirin
2 tbsp tamari
4 tsp grated ginger
4 tbsp coconut blossom nectar
coconut oil for frying

METHOD

Place the salmon fillets in a bowl and pour over the rest of the ingredients, then cover and leave in the fridge for 30 minutes (don't fret if you don't though!). Next fry each fillet in a tiny bit of coconut oil, skin side down , until the raw orangey flesh turns a pinky white, turning afterwards so that the top browns, and finally transferring to a baking dish ready to grill in a pre-heated grill. If there is any left-over marinade spoon some of it on top of the fillets before you grill them and then grill until the top caramelises and turns slightly char grilled. Serve them with buttered spinach and new potatoes.

NUTRI-FACT ✳

Omega-3 fatty acids are essential nutrients for our health and since our bodies can't make omega-3 fats, we must get them through food. One type of omega-3 fatty acids is found in fatty fish such as salmon, so it is good to include it in your diet. Some benefits of omega-3 fatty acids are protection against heart disease, irritable bowel disease and some auto-immune diseases such as lupus and rheumatoid arthritis.

Salmon Fishcakes

" Give a man fish and he has food for a day; teach him how to fish and you can get rid of him the entire weekend" (Zeena Schaffer)

INGREDIENTS (Serves 4)

4 fillets organic salmon

2 large potatoes, unpeeled and cubed

1 generous handful chopped parsley

2 tbsp organic oatmeal

1 egg

1 tbsp mayonnaise *(see recipe p. 64)*

juice of 1 lemon

coconut oil for frying

Herbamare seasoning (you can get it from health food shops and on-line)

METHOD

Pre-heat oven to 180°c. Stick the potatoes in a saucepan, cover with water, boil and cook till soft and fluffy. Pop salmon fillets into a dish and slosh over the lemon juice. Scatter well with Herbamare seasoning - there are no artificial additives or MSG in it and although its quite high in sodium, it has fresh herbs and spices. Bake for half an hour in a preheated fan oven at 180°C until only just cooked through and succulent. In a large mixing bowl flake the salmon fillets, removing the skin beforehand, and smush roughly with the boiled potatoes; add the parsley. Add the mayonnaise, egg and oatmeal and mix all ingredients until integrated. Spoon 12-ish tablespoon blobs onto a board and form each one into a ball in the palm of your hands, then flatten slightly, pressing with your hands, so that they resemble fishcakes. Heat a tablespoon of coconut oil in a pan and fry each fishcake until browned and cooked on each side (about 5 minutes per side). Serve with Homemade Tartare Sauce, or Homemade Tomato Sauce *(see recipe p. 63)*

Vegetable Quinoa

"The phytochemicals, antioxidants, and fibre - all of the healthful components of plant foods- originate in plants, not animals. If they are present, it is because animals ate plants. And why should we go through an animal to get the benefits of the plants themselves?" (Colleen Patrick-Goudreau, *Color me Vegan*)

INGREDIENTS (Serves at least 4 as a side dish)

2 of each: yellow peppers, green peppers and red peppers, cubed,

2 large red onions sliced

3 crushed garlic cloves

1 aubergine, cubed

coconut oil

olive oil

salt and pepper for seasoning

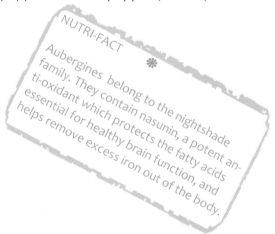

NUTRI-FACT

Aubergines belong to the nightshade family. They contain nasunin, a potent anti-oxidant which protects the fatty acids essential for healthy brain function, and helps remove excess iron out of the body.

METHOD

Grease a baking tray with coconut oil, place all the ingredients on it and season with salt and pepper. Next bake in a fan oven pre-heated to 180° C for about 45 minutes or until the vegetables have all reduced and slightly caramelised. If necessary, drain some of the water from the baking tray halfway through baking, and return to the oven for further cooking. In the meantime cook the quinoa according to the packet instructions. When the vegetables are cooked, mix them together with the cooked quinoa and serve as an accompaniment or eat on their own.

NUTRI-FACT ❀

Coconut oil or butter is best to use for frying because the other oils become unstable when they are heated (even olive oil!) and can cause health problems. So if you don't like the coconut taste much (actually you can't really taste it), use butter instead or some other saturated fat like goose fat.

Polenta or Quinoa Chicken Schnitzel

" Left wing, chicken wing, it don't make no difference to me" (Woody Guthrie)

This is a great schnitzel for Pesach.

INGREDIENTS (Serves 2 not-so-hungry-people or 1 very hungry person)

1 packet organic mini chicken fillets
1 cup polenta (replace with quinoa flakes for Pesach)
2 eggs, slightly beaten
1 cup quinoa flour seasoned with salt and pepper(quinoa flour is fine on Pesach)
coconut oil for frying

METHOD

Spin each mini fillet in the flour, then submerge into beaten egg mixture and finally coat with polenta (or quinoa). Melt the coconut oil in a frying pan over moderate heat and fry the fillets for about 10 minutes, turning occasionally to ensure they are cooked through.

My Tip: I use a temperature thermometer called a Thermapen (but Ocado also has something similar called a Metalex Meat Thermometer) to make sure poultry, meat and fish is cooked through. According to Food Health and Safety regulations, poultry is properly cooked when it reaches a temperature above 75 °C. You simply jab the needle in each fillet, which takes no time at all, and watch the temperature go up. Although it's not cheap, it's better than getting salmonella poisoning! And you will never have tasted such tender, succulent, juicy chicken schnitzels, because generally people over-cook the chicken to make sure it's cooked. This way you know exactly when and it will almost melt in your mouth!

Steamed Cod with Ginger and Spring Onion

INGREDIENTS (Serves 4)

100 g pak choi

4 x 150 g cod or other firm white fish

5 cm piece ginger, shredded

2 garlic cloves, sliced

1 tsp mirin rice wine

1 bunch spring onions, shredded

handful chopped coriander

brown basmati rice

1 lime cut into wedges

2 tbsps tamari

chilli (optional)

METHOD

Heat the oven to 180 °c. Cut a square of baking parchment big enough to make a large envelope for each fillet (so 4 envelopes in all). Place the pak choi on each one followed by the fish and then the ginger and garlic. Pour over the tamari and rice wine, then season and fold over the parchment sealing 3 edges of each. Next put on a baking sheet and cook for 20 minutes. Finally open and scatter over spring onions, coriander (and chilli if desired) and serve with brown basmati rice and lime. PS It has a rusticky feel if you serve it still in the parchment.

NUTRI-FACT

Tamari's rich flavour comes from an abundance of amino acids derived from soy protein. It contains less salt than traditional soy sauce and aids in the digestion of fruits and vegetables, while being rich in minerals. It contains little or no wheat and can be found wheat-free for people with a gluten intolerance.

Tuna "Colette" Salad

Salad "freshens without enfeebling and fortifies without irritating."
(Jean-Anthelme Brillat-Savarin, 755-1826)

We call this a Colette salad because it was my sister, Charlotte's favourite lunch at Colette when she stayed in Paris. Although my mum and I have no idea of the original recipe, we have concocted our own version which goes down very well.

INGREDIENTS (Serves 1)

1 can tuna in olive oil
1/4 each of yellow, red and green peppers chopped into 1 mm cubes
Bunch of chives thinly chopped
Salt and pepper to taste
Quick and versatile mayonnaise dressing *(see recipe p.66)*
Small iceberg lettuce hearts

METHOD

Drain the tuna and mix it with the peppers and chives in a bowl. Add some salt and pepper to taste and two dessertspoons of the mayonnaise dressing, or more or less as desired. Spoon the contents into a rounded cup and then invert onto a plate to serve, so that it looks like a mould. Slice the lettuce hearts and place them on the plate. Drizzle them with some mayonnaise dressing. We often slice some avocado and add the slices to the lettuce hearts. This is a quick and easy lunchtime recipe, which I love.

Chicken Waldorf Salad

This is another quick and easy lunchtime recipe.

INGREDIENTS (Serves 4)

1 kg cooked chicken

8 spring onions chopped

4 sticks celery chopped

50 g chopped walnuts

1 large apple thinly sliced

1 iceberg lettuce

Quick and Versatile Mayonnaise Dressing *(see recipe p.64)*

METHOD

Strip the skin from the chicken, debone it and cut it into chunks. Place these chunks in a bowl with the celery, spring onions and walnuts. Toss with the mayonnaise dressing. Using your hands fold the apple slices into the mixture. Place some lettuce leaves on each serving plate and spoon the salad on top. Add some more dressing to the lettuce leaves if desired.

Quick and Easy Cold Platter

Sometimes I like an assorted cold platter for lunch (my mum actually does this for me). She puts 2 or 3 slices of smoked salmon/ cold chicken/ some tuna on a plate. With that I have an apple cut into rings or some strawberries, some kale chips and two quinoa or buckwheat crackers or a slice of my gluten-free almond bread. That keeps me full until the evening and I really enjoy it .

Aruna's Mung Bean and Coconut Soup

This is a great way to use the water from blanching vegetables! It adds a lovely flavour to the mung beans and you don't need stock! The up side is you can create a lovely salad on the side with the vegetables you've blanched. A favourite is blanched green beans and long stem broccoli with a dressing of sesame oil, tamari soy and a sprinkling of sesame seed.

INGREDIENTS

6 cups of (lightly salted) water after blanching greens
250 g split yellow mung beans
2 tomatoes quartered
2 slices of ginger (skin on)
3 cloves of garlic, skinned up, left whole
1 green chili, whole but with a slit down the centre
1 tsp turmeric powder
1/4 cup coconut milk
1 bunch coriander leaves finely chopped

METHOD

Using the water used for blanching vegetables, add garlic, ginger, chili, turmeric. Bring to the boil. Rinse the mung beans and add to the boiling water. Bring back to the boil and then simmer on a low heat till tender (around 15 - 20 minutes). Aruna says that it's a good idea to leave a stainless steel spoon in the pot to ensure that the pot doesn't overflow. Once cooked through, add more water if it is too thick. When the required consistency is achieved, stir in the coriander leaves. At this stage you can add the coconut milk or pour the coconut milk into a serving jug for your guests to serve themselves to taste. Remember coconut milk is a great non dairy milk which can be served alongside meat dishes if you're kosher.

Chicken Chausseur

INGREDIENTS (SERVES 4)

400 g skinless and boneless chicken thighs,

1 tbsp fresh thyme leaves

1 onion, finely chopped

2 garlic cloves, crushed

1 tbsp tomato puree

1 tsp coconut blossom nectar

200 ml dry cider

200 ml organic chicken stock

300 g small chestnut mushrooms, halved

200 g tinned chopped tomatoes

2 tbsp chopped fresh flatleaf parsley, to garnish (optional)

4 servings grilled vegetable quinoa, to serve

coconut oil for frying

METHOD

Cook the chicken thighs in heated coconut oil until browned all over and transfer to a plate; add the onion and thyme to the pan and cook for 4 to 5 minutes and then the garlic and tomato puree and cook for a further 1 minute; next return the chicken to the pan, then add the coconut nectar, cider, stock, mushrooms and tomatoes and simmer. Transfer to a casserole dish, cover and bake in a fan oven pre-heated to 180 °C for 45 minutes or until extremely tender. Scatter with parsley and serve with vegetable quinoa.

NUTRI-FACT ✳

Coconut nectar comes from the coconut tree. The coconut tree is tapped and produces a nutrient rich "sap" that exudes from the coconut blossom. It is an abundant source of vitamins and a neutral PH. The sap is minimally processed at low temperature for a few hours, producing a thick sap that contains only 10% fructose.

Blanched Greens

I never really knew what 'blanching' vegetables meant and neither did my mum and then she discovered that all of us like this method of cooking them. It is better than steaming or boiling, because the vegetables are only slightly cooked and so retain all their nutrients. They are also crunchy and bright green, which makes them more tempting than that sickly brownish colour greens turn into when you over-boil or over-steam them. We boil the water in a pot until it bubbles vigorously. Then we throw in our greens……. whether these are broccoli, asparagus or green beans….whatever. We leave them to boil for about two minutes and then drain them under cold water. They are bright green and crunchy but not raw. Sometimes we melt some butter in a pan and sauté them in the butter quickly, seasoning to taste. We also sometimes add a bit of garlic to the butter and/or some chillies for a change.

Buttered Spinach

INGREDIENTS (serves 4)

1 x 500 g bag baby spinach
2 cloves garlic
coconut oil
Himalayan salt and black pepper
1 knob butter
1 lemon

NUTRI-FACT ✳
Spinach is one of the best sources of dietary potassium. It is also a good non-haeme source of iron. It is one of the best sources of dietary magnesium too.

METHOD

Wash and drain the spinach. Finely slice the garlic. Heat the pan and add coconut oil followed by the garlic. Once the garlic is golden, tip in the spinach and mix it around. Season and then tip it into a colander. Put the pan back on the hob. Add the butter. When heated return the spinach and squeeze over lemon juice. Stir and add more seasoning if necessary. Serve immediately.

Sweet Potato Chips

INGREDIENTS (Serves 3)

3 sweet potatoes, thinly sliced into rounds, skin on

1 tablespoon coconut oil for frying

Himalayan salt and pepper

paprika (optional)

METHOD

Heat the coconut oil and then add the potato rounds making sure you don't crowd them out. Fry them in batches if necessary. Turn occasionally. Once nicely golden and crisp, remove from the pan and drain on kitchen towel. Season with salt and pepper and paprika, if desired.

NUTRI-FACT ✳
Sweet potatoes are high in antioxidants and are an excellent source of carbohydrates for those with blood sugar problems. They are rich in fibre and are excellent for those who are pregnant because they are high in folate.

Cinnamon Spiced Roasted Butternut

INGREDIENTS (Serves 4)

1 large butternut, peeled, seeded and cut into 1-inch cubes

1 tablespoon coconut oil

1 tablespoon coconut palm sugar

1/2 teaspoon ground cinnamon

1 teaspoon Himalayan salt

dash cayenne

METHOD

Heat the oven to 200 ° C. Toss the butternut cubes with coconut oil, palm sugar, cinnamon, salt and cayenne until well coated. Tumble the cubes onto 2 large baking sheets and spread into 1 layer. Don't crowd them out. Roast the squash, turning until the edges are browned, about 45 minutes.

> NUTRI-FACT ✳
>
> Butternut squash is loaded with antioxidant carotenoids to protect your body's cells from damaging free radicals.

Baby New Potatoes

INGREDIENTS (Serves 4)
About 16 new potatoes, the smaller the better
1/2 tablespoon of butter
Himalayan salt

METHOD
Boil or steam the new potatoes until tender but 'al dente'. Drain them in a colander and then return them to the pan. Spoon the butter into the potatoes. Season as desired and serve.

Brown Basmati Rice

Cook according to the packet instructions, add a blob of butter and season if desired.

> NUTRI-FACT ✳
>
> Basmati is a non-glutinous rice. Brown basmati, being less processed than white , keeps its wholegrain, nutritional value. It also provides twice the fibre of white. Basmati has the highest content of all rice of essential nutrients, such as manganese, magnesium and vitamin B, and amino acids.

Homemade Tomato Sauce

"Three tomatoes are walking down the street- a papa tomato, a mama tomato and a little baby tomato. Baby tomato starts lagging behind. Papa tomato gets angry, goes over to Baby tomato and squishes him ...and says " Ketchup!" (Uma Thurman in *Pulp Fiction*, 1994)

INGREDIENTS

2 400 g cans chopped tomatoes

2 tbsp coconut oil

2 chopped shallots

3 chopped garlic cloves

2 tbsp tomato purée

salt and ground black pepper

2 tbsp white wine vinegar

3 tbsp coconut palm sugar

NURTI-FACT ❋

Tomatoes have lycopene – the compound that gives it its red colour. It has potent anti-cancerous activity. When cooked the bioavailability of lycopene increases rather than decreases so you are better off eating tomatoes cooked than raw. So your best bet is to make your own tomato sauce from scratch like this one rather than to eat raw tomatoes.

METHOD

Heat the 2 tablespoon oil in a pan. Add the shallots and garlic cloves and cook gently for 5 minutes or until softened. Stir in the tomato purée, fry for 30 seconds, then stir in the cans of chopped tomatoes. Bring to the boil and bubble for 20 minutes or until most of the liquid has evaporated. Cool slightly, then whiz in a blender or food processor until smooth. Return to the clean pan, season with salt and ground black pepper, then add the coconut palm sugar and white wine vinegar. Bring to boil and simmer for 2-3 minutes, then cool. Refrigerate for up to 3 days.

Homemade Mayonnaise

"Mayonnaise is France's gift to the New World's muddled palate, a boon that combines humanity's ancient instinctive craving for the cellular warmth of pure fat with the modern, romantic fondness for complex flavours. Mayo (as the lazy call it) may appear mild and prosaic, but behind its creamy veil it fairly seethes with tangy disposition" (Tom Robbins, *Villa Incognito*)

INGREDIENTS

1 large egg
juice of 1/2 of 1 lemon
1/4 teaspoon salt
1 cup extra light tasting olive oil

NUTRI-FACT ✱
This recipe has raw egg, so do not serve it to the vulnerable (the very young or elderly) or people with compromised immune systems.

EQUIPMENT
Immersion blender
Tall, narrow glass jar, just wide enough to accommodate the head of the blender

METHOD

Add all the ingredients to the glass jar and leave for a few seconds to allow the egg to settle at the bottom of the jar. Push the head of the blender right to the bottom of the jar so it touches it and turn on the power. Do not move the blender for 20 seconds. You will see the oil emulsify and turn into a creamy thick concoction, making its way to the top of the jar. After 20 seconds move the blender around to incorporate every last bit of oil. Store in an airtight container in the fridge for up to two weeks.

Homemade Tartare Sauce

" Confidence is going after Moby Dick in a rowboat and taking the tartare sauce with you" (Zig Ziglar)

INGREDIENTS

1 tbsp gherkins finally chopped
1 tbsp capers finally chopped
3 tbsp flatleaf parsley
2 medium organic eggs
1 tsp xylitol
1 tsp grainy mustard
350 ml sunflower oil
squeeze of lemon juice

METHOD

Chop 1 tablespoon gherkins and capers finely, along with 3 tablespoons flatleaf parsley. Crack and separate 2 medium, organic eggs, and chuck the yolks (keep the whites for meringues...not so naughty if you use xylitol instead of sugar...it really works but tastes a bit like sugar-free chewing gum) in a bowl with 1 teaspoon grainy mustard, and whisk together. Very gradually whisk in 350 ml sunflower oil to make a mayonnaise (by the end it will be too thick to whisk). Whack in a good squeeze of lemon juice then fold in the chopped parsley, capers and gherkins. Serve with the fishcakes.

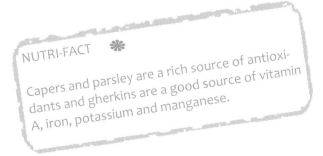

NUTRI-FACT

Capers and parsley are a rich source of antioxidants and gherkins are a good source of vitamin A, iron, potassium and manganese.

Quick and Versatile Mayonnaise Dressing

INGREDIENTS

1 dessertspoon white balsamic vinegar
2 tbsp my mayonnaise *(see recipe p.64)*
2 dessertspoons full fat Greek yoghurt (for a dressing with a meat dish, if you are kosher, omit the yoghurt - it will still taste good)
2 tsp chopped tarragon
2 cloves garlic, crushed
1 tsp salt
black pepper to taste

METHOD
Whizz all ingredients together in a blender and dress the salads as desired.

Cakes and Desserts

Why not try?

I've got a sweet tooth and definitely like my cakes and desserts. I don't eat them every day but usually about 4 x a week which would be a bit much if they were regular desserts but since these are all made with sugar substitutes and healthy fats, I haven't found it a problem indulging as often as I do. It's hard for me to pick but try make and freeze (although everything lasts quite well in air-tight containers).

Carrot Cake

"Let them eat cake" (Marie Antoinette)

INGREDIENTS

200 g coconut oil
200 g xylitol
200 g quinoa flour
1 tsp baking powder
200 g ground walnuts
200 g chopped walnuts
4 medium carrots
8 medium eggs

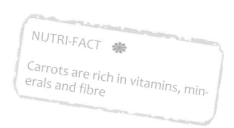

NUTRI-FACT ✳

Carrots are rich in vitamins, minerals and fibre

ICING
200 g Philadelphia cream cheese
1 tsp vanilla
4 tsp xylitol
handful chopped walnuts

METHOD

Pre-heat the oven to 180 ° C and line a cake tin with baking parchment. Cream the oil and xylitol together until smooth and then stir in the flour, baking powder and ground walnuts till the mixture becomes "breadcrumby". Add the chopped walnuts and carrots and then fold in the eggs. Spoon into the prepared tin and bake for at least 20 minutes before taking it out and covering with foil. Then immediately bake for at least another 20 minutes or until a knife inserted in the middle comes out clean. It may be that it has to stay in the oven for quite a bit longer...it definitely can't be runny inside when you take it out. It must be firm, but don't worry because once covered it wont burn. Allow it to cool completely before icing it. To make the icing, mix all the ingredients together and spread on top of the cake. Then sprinkle with chopped nuts.

Baked Apples and Almond Custard

" On the other hand...I adore stewed apples..." (La Grande Bouffe 1973)

INGREDIENTS

4 Bramley cooking apples, cored
and cut in half horizontally,
unpeeled
4 tbsp flaked almonds

FOR THE ALMOND CUSTARD
2 tbsp cornflour
420 ml water
2 heaped tbsp ground almonds
2 tbsp xylitol

NUTRI-FACT ✳

The phytonutrients in apples can help you regulate your blood sugar levels. Apple polyphenols can help prevent spikes in blood sugar through a variety of mechanisms.

METHOD

Pre-heat the oven to 180 ° C and place apples on a baking tray. Bake for 20 minutes until soft, but not too soft, basically 'al dente'. Meanwhile fry the flaked almonds in a pan until golden and then set aside. For the custard, mix the cornflour with as much water as you need to make it smooth. Pour it into a pan with the ground almonds and xylitol and heat gently, stirring and gradually adding the rest of the water to form a smooth, thick sauce.

Top each apple half with the custard or you can use cashew nut cream instead *(seer recipe p. 22)* and then sprinkle with the flaked almonds and serve.

Aunty Freda's Cheesecake

" You have to be a romantic to invest yourself, your money and your time in cheese" (Anthony Bourdain)

INGREDIENTS FOR THE BASE

20 of my ginger oat cookies (see recipe p. 29) or as many that will fill the base of a springform cake tin (or oven-proof pie dish) when mixed with the butter 125 g (or more if required) butter, melted.

METHOD

Crush the cookies with your fingertips and squish them up with the butter to make a crumbed consistency . Then mould into the base of the springform cake tin and along the sides but only about an inch up the side of the tin (the cheese-cake will set itself so there is no need to encase it all.) Then add the filling and bake for 45 minutes or until golden on top and firmly set in the middle (if it wob-bles when you move the cake tin, it's not ready.) If you need to cook it longer, cover the top with foil so that it doesn't burn. After you've removed it from the oven, let it cool completely and then refrigerate for an hour before removing it from the springform tin

INGREDIENTS FOR THE FILLING

750 g cream cheese
250 ml cream
3 separated eggs , 1 extra egg white
3/4 cup of xylitol
full desert spoon quinoa flour
full desert spoon custard powder (or corn flour)
1 tbsp brandy
1 tbsp lemon juice

METHOD

Mix all ingredients together EXCEPT ALL THE EGG WHITES then beat egg whites till fluffy and then add to mixture, gently folding them in. Pour into pre-made biscuit base and put in oven and cool as directed above.

My mum's Free-From Chocolate Cake

"Momma always said life is like a box of chocolates. You never know what you're gonna get". *(Forrest Gump)*

INGREDIENTS

4 eggs, separated (keep both yolks and whites!!)

120 g xylitol (or other natural sweetener like stevia, to taste)

160 g dark chocolate (at least 70-80% cocoa solids)

160 g butter, cut into cubes

160 g ground almonds

assorted essences (e.g., coffee, orange, etc. and play around and find good combinations) to taste (optional)

METHOD

Preheat the oven to 200 ° C (180° fan). Chop the chocolate into pieces and melt in a bowl over a saucepan of boiling water on the stove (or in a microwave, but if using a microwave put it in for NO MORE than 30 seconds then stir till melted). Cut butter into cubes and add to the melted chocolate and stir till melted. While melting the chocolate, beat the egg whites till stiff, and then slowly beat in the sugar (xylitol). When the butter and chocolate has melted, stir in the egg yolks and mix well. Then fold the chocolate mixture into the egg whites. Lastly fold in the ground almonds. This is the stage that, if you want to, you can add in various essences and play around with it and see what works. Put into the buttered and lined tin (or just buttered if springform) and bake for 20 minutes, before taking it out and covering with foil so the top doesn't burn. Return it to the oven (covered) for another 25 minutes, or until a knife inserted in the middle comes out clean. It should be springy in the centre. Leave to cool, and decorate with raspberries and a sprig of mint if desired.

> NUTRI-FACT ✱
>
> Quality dark chocolate with a high cocoa content contains antioxidants such as polyphenols and flavanols which can improve blood flow in the arteries and blood flow to the skin, protecting it from sun damage. But it is still loaded with calories. A square or two after dinner is enough.

Hazelnut and Chocolate Mousse

" I think I do myself a disservice by comparing myself to Steve Jobs and Walt Disney and human beings that were seen before. I should be more like Willy Wonka...and welcome to my chocolate factory." (Kanye West)

INGREDIENTS (Serves 4)

150 g 85% dark chocolate, broken into chunks
100 g ground hazelnuts
4 organic free range eggs, separated

METHOD

Melt the chocolate in a saucepan over heat (i.e. put the chunks in a small pyrex dish that fits into the rim of a saucepan that is 1/4 filled with boiling water, stirring it from time to time). Remove the bowl from the heat and gently stir in the hazelnuts and the 4 egg yolks, 1 at a time. Whisk the egg whites until they form peaks (so stiff that if you turn the bowl upside down they wont fall out...). Use a metal spoon so that the air doesn't escape from the beaten egg...take 1 spoonful at a time and fold into the mixture, being careful not to lose air. Spoon into a bowl or individual ramekins and allow to set in the fridge for at least an hour.

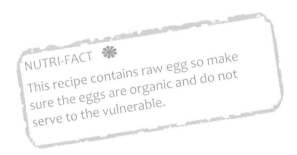

NUTRI-FACT ✳
This recipe contains raw egg so make sure the eggs are organic and do not serve to the vulnerable.

Blueberry Pear Crumble

"I'll be back before you can say Blueberry pie" (Bruce Willis)

INGREDIENTS

8 ripe pears, cored and diced
6 medium-sized punnets of blueberries
1 tsp ground cinnamon
1 tablespoon orange juice
4 tsp xylitol

METHOD

Place the fruit in a saucepan with the cinnamon, orange juice and xylitol. Cover and stew until the fruit softens, stirring occasionally to prevent sticking. Once cooked, spoon into an ovenproof dish and cover with my granola as a topping.

Dot with butter, and bake in an oven pre-heated to 180 °C until the topping has browned and the fruit mixture has bubbled through it.

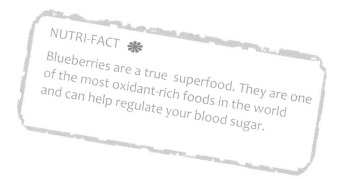

NUTRI-FACT ✳
Blueberries are a true superfood. They are one of the most oxidant-rich foods in the world and can help regulate your blood sugar.

Roasted Fruit

A really simple and delicious dessert

INGREDIENTS

4 large fresh figs,
4 large nectarines,
4 large peaches,
4 clementines,
4 large plums,
coconut blossom nectar and Himalayan salt to drizzle

METHOD

Cut all the fruit into large chunks and place into a baking tray, mixing them roughly with your hands to ensure an even spread of different fruit. Squeeze coconut blossom nectar generously over the fruit and sprinkle over Himalayan salt, amalgamating with your hands. Roast in an oven pre-heated to 200 °c for ½ an hour or until softened and slightly caramelised but still 'al dente'. Serve with Cashew Cream *(see recipe p. 22)*

Vanilla Ice Cream

"Forget art. Put your trust in ice cream."
(Charles Baxter, The Feast of Love)

This is a very nice base recipe, so play around with it. You do need an ice-cream maker and they're not that expensive - look for something on-line.

INGREDIENTS

250 ml whole milk
 125 ml double cream
1 vanilla pod, split lengthways
2 egg yolks
90 xylitol
pinch of sea salt

METHOD

Put the milk and cream in a saucepan. Split vanilla pod by running a knife down it. Scrape the seeds into the milk and cream, followed by the empty pod. Heat gently, and stir until steamed. Whisk egg yolks in heatproof bowl until smooth. Add sugar (xylitol), and salt, and whisk till pale and fluffy. Pour hot milk into egg mixture, while whisking constantly to prevent eggs scrambling. Return mixture to saucepan, and put over low heat, again, stirring constantly, till the mixture thickens into a custard and thinly coats the back of a wooden spoon. Leave custard to cool for 20-30 minutes. Put into an ice cream maker.
My Tip: I store my ice-cream maker in a freezer when I'm not using it so that it's ready to use when I need it.

 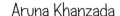

images bound to last

www.openandshutltd.com

Aruna Khanzada expresses her passion for food and photography in the same vein as this book: honest, natural and wholesome. She is excited by the amazing properties of herbs and spices and how their medicinal and nutritional value can be combined to create interesting culinary experiences without the need of artificial additives and processes to heighten the taste. Her photography follows this ethos: natural light and capturing the reality of the moment without any airbrushing!